# Finding Out About
# LIFE IN BRITAIN
# IN THE 1920s

# Monica Hodgson

B.T. Batsford Limited,  *London*

# Contents

**Frontispiece**
Family tea in 1920.

**Cover illustrations**
The colour print is a Southern Railway poster by Crawthorn, showing the seafront at Brighton (*Royal Pavilion Art Gallery and Museums*); the black and white print shows a queue of men outside a London labour exchange waiting for the dole; the right-hand print is the front cover of the programme of the first Cup Final, held in the Wembley Stadium on 28 April 1923 (*Wembley Historical Society*).

© Monica Hodgson 1987
First published 1987

Typeset by Tek-Art Ltd, Kent
and printed in Great Britain by
R J Acford Ltd,
Chichester, Sussex
for the publishers
B.T. Batsford Limited,
4 Fitzhardinge Street
London W1H 0AH

ISBN 0 7134 5156 4

**ACKNOWLEDGMENTS**

The Author and Publishers would like to thank the following for permission to reproduce illustrations: BBC Hulton Picture Library for pages 13, 23, 25, 35 and 39 (top); Bodleian Library, Oxford, for page 19; Condé Nast Publications for page 3; Mary Evans Picture Library for page 42; Imperial War Museum for page 6; J.M. Rawcliffe for pages 11 (right) and 39 (bottom) (Bill Moreton); Royal Aeronautical Society for page 29 (bottom); J. Sainsbury p.l.c. for pages 14 and 36; Science Museum for page 29 (top); Wembley Historical Society for pages 31 and 33. The map on page 44 was drawn by Matthew Ralph.

# Introduction

The Twenties were not so long ago and there are still people who can remember those days. Your grandparents may have been alive then, and may be able to tell you what life was like for a child at that time. This might help you to understand how different life is for you 60 years later.

It was not an easy time in which to grow up. Conflict with Germany had ended on 11 November 1918, only 13 months before the decade began, and the years that followed the most terrible war in our history were not the most stirring or exciting. They were difficult; they were also interesting, as so many changes were taking place in the way people lived and what they did with their lives.

One of the most obvious changes was in the behaviour of younger people. Their new attitudes and altered lifestyle gave a special character to the Twenties. The war years had brought hardship and tragedy to many families, but it had also swept away many of the restraints on the behaviour of young people. When the war ended at last, and life could be enjoyed again, they found that they were able to do so in ways which had not been allowed to their parents.

Young women, in particular, were able to live very different lives from those their mothers had lived. They smoked in public, using long cigarette holders, they cut off their hair and shortened their skirts, they wore make-up and went to parties unchaperoned. None of these things had been acceptable before the war.

All classes of society, except the very poorest, were affected by these changes, but it was the sons and daughters of the wealthy and aristocratic leaders of society who set the standard, with their fast cars and their casual clothes. They went to weekend parties where they played tennis and danced the Charleston to the music of jazz bands. Their leader was the charming and popular young Prince of Wales, the eldest son of the King, George V.

Even the role of the monarchy was changing. George V's reign began before the First World War, and ended three years before the Second. The popularity of his son, whose photograph appeared in all the newspapers, and the new technology of the Twenties – the motor car and the radio – were bringing the King into closer contact with his people. When he opened the great Empire Exhibition at Wembley in 1924, the people were able to hear for the first time the voice of their King speaking directly to them. The Christmas Day broadcasts to the

*One of the hallmarks of the Twenties:* Vogue *fashion magazine. This is the front cover of the April 1927 edition, designed by Benito.*

people of Britain, still made every year by Queen Elizabeth II, were instituted by her grandfather, King George V.

These things helped to strengthen the position of the Crown by arousing the interest and loyalty of the British people, a loyalty which was increased by the way the King and members of the Royal Family played their part in the life of the nation. The wedding of the King's only daughter, the Princess Mary, to the Earl of Harwood in 1923 became a day of celebration for the whole nation.

Changes were also taking place in the way we were governed. For the first time in our history a political party representing the interests of working people was voted into office. In 1924 the Labour party, under the leadership of Ramsey MacDonald, was asked to form a government. Without previous experience of holding office, and dependent upon the votes of the Liberal party for support, it was not able to deal very successfully with the economic problems with which the country was faced. The Socialists were unable to do as much as they would have liked for the working people who had voted for them, many of whom were kept poor by low wages and unemployment. A start had been made in the building of council houses, but not enough was done, and in the general election a few months later they were replaced by a Conservative government under the leadership of Stanley Baldwin. During his prime ministership unemployment continued to escalate and he had to face the nine-day General Strike of 1926.

In 1929 The Labour party was returned to office again, with a clear majority of seats in the House of Commons, but by then the country was sliding into the slump – known as the Great Depression – that was to characterize much of the Thirties.

Before the war many of the things we take for granted – gas and electricity to light and heat our homes, telephones and radios, motor cars and many other things which make our lives easy and comfortable – were much too expensive for all but the wealthy. But, after the war, factories using new machinery and new methods of production were able to turn out many more goods at prices ordinary people could afford. This led to many changes in the lives of ordinary people; it affected the kind of house they lived in and where it was built; it affected the kind of work they did, where they went to work and how they travelled there; it increased the amount of spare time they had and altered how they spent it; it gave people more goods to buy and more shops to buy them in.

As we have seen, women were experiencing a new freedom in the Twenties and their position in society was also changing. Though not all women were able to take advantage of this, real advances were made. For the first time women were able to vote in the elections, and in 1920 Lady Astor took her seat in the House of Commons, the first woman ever to do so. Many more women were able to become doctors, lawyers, university teachers and civil servants. Improved education allowed them to play a more active part in our national life.

All these changes made Britain a rather restless place. People moved from one part of the country to another in search of work, a better job or a new home. It was a time of strikes and demonstrations by those who felt they were being shut out of benefits of this new society. People went further away for their holidays and spent their free time at the cinema and at football matches.

Financially and economically the Twenties were difficult years but, despite this, the changes taking place were making life easier for many people, and by 1929 it looked as if the worst was over and there was hope for the future. But, in November of that year, the American banking system collapsed, bringing great hardship to the Americans themselves and to all those countries which depended on loans from the United States. So, despite the many improvements the Twenties had brought to the lives of British people, the decade did not, after all, end on a cheerful note.

# Useful Sources

If you are interested in finding out more about your own town or village there are a number of ways of obtaining information.

## 1. PEOPLE

There are still people alive who grew up in the Twenties. Your grandparents or other elderly relatives, neighbours and friends may be able to help you with their memories of the time. A tape recorder is a useful way of recording this information.

Your teachers may be able to help with old photographs or papers. Perhaps you might be able to see the school log book.

Your local librarian may be able to help with copies of old newspapers, maps and directories.

If there is a local history society in your district it may have materials that would help to build up a record of local events.

## 2. BUILDINGS

With a little practice you should be able to identify buildings which date from the Twenties. Rows of semi-detached houses, factories and cinemas are the most common. Maps from the reference library will help you to identify the areas which were developed in the Twenties. Find out when the council estates in your area were built — after the First or Second World War?

## 3. VISUAL MATERIALS

a) *Old photographs* These are a valuable source of information. Most families have some hidden away somewhere. Your local reference library may have a collection of photographs; so may the local newspaper if it was published in the Twenties.

b) *Objects* Domestic tools, ornaments and jewellery will probably be found in the local history museum, or if you know what to look for you may find them in the local antique or junk shop. Your grandparents may even have some ornaments and clocks which date from the period. The Science Museum in London has a collection of domestic articles, such as vacuum-cleaners, radiators and lighting appliances. They also have vehicles of various kinds. Postcards, stamps and copies of magazines can sometimes be found in junk shops.

## 4. WRITTEN SOURCES

a) *Reference books* Try your local history or reference library. You may not find many that are specially about the Twenties but any history of Britain between the wars will have some material from these years.

b) *Fiction* Many novels have been written about the Twenties and many were published during the decade. Look at the date of first publication inside the front cover. Look out for authors such as Michael Arlen, E.F. Benson, Aldous Huxley and Evelyn Waugh.

c) *Autobiographies* There are a number of autobiographies which contain material from the Twenties. Some are written by famous people, others by ordinary people looking back on their childhood. Some of these have been listed for you at the back of this book.

d) *Directories and guides* These are a useful source of information about the growth of your town or village. Directories like *Kelly's* will give help in finding out what shops and businesses were in existence 60 years ago. See how many of these still exist.

e) *Documents and Records* If you are particularly interested in some development — health, housing or education, for example — you can look up speeches made in Parliament in *Hansard*. This is not easy to read, but is an important source if you are doing any serious research. All sorts of information can usually be obtained from the County Archives, where minutes of local council meetings, parish meetings and education affairs can be consulted.

f) *Newspapers and Magazines* Copies of old newspapers and magazines can often be seen in reference libraries. These give interesting accounts of the lives of the Royal Family and famous people such as film stars, and recount national events, sports fixtures and disasters of all kinds.

# After the War Was Over

The Great War, which ended on 11 November, 1918, brought many changes and created many problems for the British people which had not been solved by 1920. Although a peace treaty with defeated Germany and her allies had been signed in the summer of 1919, in Britain the war was not officially declared at an end until 31 August 1921. Men who had been called up to fight "for the duration" were given their pay until this date but there were many difficulties in settling the millions of soldiers who had fought in the war back into the post-war world.

*King George V laying a wreath at the foot of the Cenotaph, the memorial set up to remember the 750,000 men who lost their lives in the Great War, which ended on 11 November 1918. Remembrance Day is still commemorated on the first or second Sunday of November every year. What flower has become a symbol of this day?*

## ARMISTICE DAY IN THE VILLAGE

When the war ended almost every town and village in Britain set up a memorial to those who had died in the conflict. A service was – and still is – usually held there every year on 11 November.

Edward Short, who grew up to become a Member of Parliament and served as Minister of Education after the Second World War, remembers the ceremony in his own little village in Cumbria:

> **We always held a service of remembrance at the war memorial with the vicar officiating in his overlong surplice [loose white gown worn by clergy of the Church of England]. Mr Kirby, our schoolmaster, being an ex-serviceman himself, marched us there with military precision. It was a great occasion with the gentry and most of the village folk huddled round looking very sad and shivering in the cold. We children tried hard to be as solemn as the rest and thought about the jaunty young men who had gone off to the war with a fag in the corner of their mouths and a kit bag over their shoulders; many of them never to return.** (Edward Short, *I Knew My Place*, 1983)

Is there a war memorial near you? You may find it in the churchyard or the centre of the village. Count the names. It will tell you how many young men from the village were killed in the First World War.

## ARTIFICIAL LIMBS FOR 40,000 MEN

When the war was over thousands of blind and crippled men were in need of help to restore their shattered lives. This account from a magazine shows one effort made in 1922.

> **Lieutenant General Sir Edward Bethune presided on Saturday at the first Annual General Meeting of the Disabled Ex-Servicemen's Association, held at the Bishopsgate Institute. The main object of the society, Sir Edward said, was to make the men feel that they were not crippled. Over 250 men attended the meeting and were entertained by a musical programme. Captain H.S. Baird said that as a result of the establishment of the society 40,000 men had been fitted with artificial limbs.** (Quoted in *Women's Times*, January 1922)

Can you think of any way in which these men who had been disabled in the war might be helped to feel they were not crippled?

## THAT DREADFUL FIRST WORLD WAR

Some ex-servicemen suffered great hardship after the war, especially if they were disabled. It was a common sight to see them selling matches on the street corner, sometimes even begging. Grace Hayward, who lived at Ore village, near Hastings, remembers them coming to her house.:

> **Mother was a very kind woman. After the dreadful first war they came up by and used to stand outside your gate and sing. They were so poverty-struck, those that had gone and fought for us . . . or else they would stand and scrape on a little, old fiddle.**
> **They'd lost arms, been blinded, they were begging, selling matches. They** used to stand about playing an old accordian, standing on one leg. Those poor men. My dad knew them all. They would have been those who went when he did. (Hastings Modern History Workshop, *Hastings Voices*, 1982)

After the First World War not all ex-servicemen could claim a pension, even if they were disabled. After the Second World War, which ended in 1945, much better care was taken of wounded soldiers, and a sad scene such as this would have been most unlikely.

## LOOKING FOR JOBS

Finding jobs for all the soldiers returning from the war was not easy and many people suffered hardship before they found work. Barbara Cartland was one of the "Bright Young Things" of that time: She remembers what life was like in 1920.

> **London was filled with men with magnificent war records and empty pockets. I have seen them in queues outside factories, hoping to be taken on; I have found them wandering into fashionable restaurants just before lunch, hoping to find someone who will offer them a meal. Every businessman has piles of letters of application hoping for a vacancy. In the country chicken farms, wayside cafés and garages have sprung up like mushrooms – all run by ex-servicemen. Many of these have already gone bankrupt and their owners have joined the patient queues of hollow-eyed men . . . waiting for a job.** (Barbara Cartland, *I Seek the Miraculous*, 1978)

Look up the word "bankrupt" on page 45 if you do not already know what it means. Can you think why so many cafés, garages and chicken farms should have failed?

# A Divided Nation

For working people living in the industrial areas of the north of England, Scotland and South Wales the Twenties was a time of hardship and distress, as many factories in Britain's traditional industries – such as cotton, coal, iron and steel – were forced to close down.

In the Midlands and the South, however, the opening of electrically powered factories to manufacture new products such as cars, vacuum-cleaners and electric light bulbs resulted in more jobs, better working conditions and higher wages for many other workers. Britain in the Twenties was a divided nation.

## IN GLASGOW

Glasgow, on the banks of the river Clyde in Scotland, was a great ship-building area, but by 1922 yards were closing and thousands of men were thrown out of work. One of them, Robert Mitchell, described Glasgow at that time.

> **I'd been working in the shipyards for seven years; then I became redundant. In Glasgow it was terrible. Street corners where men were just standing about wondering whatever dead-end job they could pick up. People were prepared to do anything to get a wee bit extra for the sake of the kids. The dole I had was 29 shillings a week for a wife and two children. After two years of drawing the dole, I took a job as a steward on a ship sailing from Glasgow to New York during the emigration period. Between 1921 and 1925, there were 635,000 people who emigrated from Britain; over a quarter of a million left in 1923 alone.** (Quoted in Lesley Baily and C.H. Brewer, eds., *BBC Scrapbook for 1923*, 1937)

See if you can find out more about emigration during this period. Do you think those who went to America would have found the life so much easier?

## THE MARCH ON LONDON

The first Hunger March, as it was called, was organized in 1922. Thousands of men from the north of England, South Wales and Scotland marched on foot all the way to London to draw the attention of the government to their plight. A nurse from one of the London hospitals watched them go by.

> **We stood in Oxford Street on Monday to watch the procession of unemployed, when thousands of men of all ages, closely guarded by the police, marched from the Embankment to Marble Arch. It was a terrible, heart-rending sight. Shivering in their poor clothes, they did not seem to have a superfluous ounce of flesh amongst them.** (*The British Journal of Nursing*, 18 February 1922)

Look up the word "superfluous" in the back of the book, if you do not know it. What does this tell you about the condition of these men who had walked all the way from Scotland, from Tyneside and from South Wales?

## NEW INDUSTRIES

While traditional industries in the North and in South Wales were laying off workers, new industries were springing up in the Midlands and in the South round London. The *Daily Telegraph* reported on 9 January 1920:

> By the side of the river Thames, near Woolwich, a factory is arising which indicates a new spirit of industry. The estimated cost of the work is £400,000. In a year the factory will be producing bottles at the rate of 100,000 per annum, using an American automatic machine.

And in November 1922, the year of the Hunger March, the *Countryside Review* described a new electrical engineering works in Bedford:

> The well-equipped works of the Igranic Electric Company vies in importance with any similar concern in the country. The works covers a large area . . . the various shops and departments are, for the most part, light and spacious . . . such conditions make for efficiency, and are indeed necessary for the health and welfare of the employees, in which a great interest is taken by the firm. . .

## THE BIGGEST THRILL

For those with wealth and leisure the world was a different place. In the year of the hunger march C.V. Buckley took a voyage on a liner. In *Good Times at Home and Abroad*, published in 1979, he describes the trip:

One of the first "new" products to be mass-produced in modern factories in the Midlands was the motor car. This is the production line in William Morris' factory in 1929.

> Of the voyages I have taken perhaps the voyage on the Cunard liner *Mauritania* in 1922 gave me the biggest thrill. To find the ballrooms, vast restaurants, passengers of every nationality, looking as if they had stepped out of the fashion magazines, was dazzling. I had never expected to find it all so vast – swimming pools, gymnasia, turkish-baths, shops, libraries, hairdressers; in fact a floating hotel. The stewards and stewardesses on the British liner were considered to be the finest in the world for efficiency, perfect good manners and kindness.

◁ *A demonstration of strikers and unemployed in Glasgow, 1919. Industrial towns in Scotland, the north of England and South Wales were particularly badly hit by unemployment.*

Find out whether this division between different parts of our country still exists. How much have things changed since 1922?

# General Strike

On 4 May, 1926 over a million British workers stopped work in support of the miners, who were in dispute with the mine owners over pay and working hours. The strike lasted nine days. By calling on volunteers, the government was able to keep essential food and services going and maintain law and order. By 12 May the strike was over. It had achieved nothing. The miners stayed on strike until November, when hunger and want drove them back to work on the owners' terms.

## THE VOICE OF A MINER

The miners' long struggle against the employers caused great hardship in many coalmining districts, but in this Yorkshire pit village a miner tells how they managed to survive without wages.

> I was twenty when the strike of 1926 was on. When the mine owners refused extra wages we just saw red. There was the threat of even longer hours. We had no strike pay. We managed by sharing everything we had. My father had a horse and cart and we went round the village collecting meat and bones from the butchers' shops. We set up soup kitchens in the village, taking all the poor children standing around, even if they weren't pit folk. Nearly everyone grew vegetables and, since our village was nearly all miners, nobody suffered starvation. (Gerard Noel, *The Great Lock-Out Of 1926*, 1972)

## NEWS DURING THE STRIKE

There were no national newspapers during the strike, though the government published a daily paper, *The British Gazette*. The BBC wireless news bulletins became very important in letting people know what was going on. Not everyone had a wireless so notices were posted in shop windows where people could read them. Advice was given in local newspapers, which were still being printed. The following appeared in the *Hastings Observer*:

## DO'S FOR DIFFICULT DAYS

*The British Worker*, a news sheet published by the Trade Union Strike Committee, gave advice to the men on strike. The following appeared on 7 May 1926:

> Do all you can to keep everyone smiling. The way to do this is to keep smiling yourself.
> Do your best to avoid any ideas of violent or disorderly conduct.
> Do things that need to be done. This will occupy you and steady your nerves if they get shaky.
> Do any odd jobs that need doing about the house.
> Do a little to interest and amuse the kiddies now you have the chance.
> Do what you can to improve your health. A good walk every day will help to keep you fit.
> Do something. Hanging about swapping stories is bad.

What does this passage tell you about the union leaders who were running the strike?

> Don't purchase more food than you really need or would normally do.
> Don't bank up the fire too often.
> Don't burn the midnight oil, or the gas.
> Don't lay down the law to all and sundry.
> Don't be scared. Be careful. —

## KEEPING THE TRAINS RUNNING

Nearly all the railway workers came out on strike, so there were few trains. As a result of an appeal by the government many young people from the middle and upper classes came forward to help. Students, engineers, even the Bright Young Things, worked to keep things going.

> **The passenger train which arrived here at 3 p.m. on Monday afternoon, after a three hour journey from Charing Cross, had the name "Betty Baldwin" painted on the side of the engine; a graceful tribute to the Prime Minister's daughter. From the roof of the cab floated a small Union Jack. The driver was a mining engineer; his fireman, a mechanical engineer and the guard was a medical student who wore plus-fours.** (*Hastings and St Leonards Observer*, 8 May 1926)

With whom, do you think, were the newspapers in sympathy?

By using volunteers like this detachment of special mounted police the government was able to maintain law and order and to prevent serious outbreaks of violence during the General Strike of 1926. How can you tell they are not regular policemen?

## WHAT WONDERFUL PEOPLE WE ARE

When the General Strike came to an end King George V wrote the following in his diary.

> **Our old country can well be proud of itself as during the last nine days there has been a strike by which four million people have been affected; not a shot has been fired and no one killed. It shows what a wonderful people we are.** (*Diary of King King George V*, 12 May 1926)

Most British people would have agreed with the King. Can you think of any group of people who might not have felt quite like that?

# HE "BRITISH GAZETTE" AND ITS OBJECTS

## Reply to Strike Makers' Plan to Paralyse Public Opinion

## EAL MEANING OF THE STRIKE

## Conflict Between Trade Union Leaders and Parliament

◁ Part of the front page of The British Gazette, *5 May 1926. Contemporary newspapers provide valuable sources of information about specific periods. Do you think the strikers would have agreed with the opinions expressed in this paper?*

11

# Homes Fit for Heroes

## COUNCIL HOUSES

By the Housing Act of 1920, the government gave money to local councils to build houses for people who could not afford to pay high rents. This extract from a debate on housing on 13 February 1920 shows how urgent the need was.

> **The primary object of this Bill is to secure ... the building of working-class houses. Every member of the House of Commons must have been moved by the constant appeals from all sections of the community and all parts of the country to do whatever is within our power to rescue our people from the appalling conditions in which they live today.**

As a result of this Act many working-class people were rehoused and lived in better conditions than they ever had done before, with more space, proper supplies of gas and water, and even a bathroom. This report from the industrial town of St Helens in Lancashire shows how much the chance of a council house meant to people.

One of the biggest problems when the war ended was to find houses for everyone. During the war few had been built, many were badly in need of repair and in the large cities too many families still lived in dirty, overcrowded conditions. It was estimated that by 1920, 8000 houses needed to be built.

> **The Council was very good – it built very good houses. ... The standard was very high. They had some first-class supervisory staff. The Clerk of the Works, who had been a builder himself, was on the job all day long. The queues for the houses were miles long. Everyone put their names on the list. They were made and jumped for joy if they got a Council house.**

How can you tell that the person writing was a building worker?

*A typical council estate. Each house is the same, but the families have an open front garden where they can grow what they like. Notice the car in the right of the picture.*

## FLATS INSTEAD OF HOUSES

Cuts in money for building meant that there were too few houses to meet the need. As late as 1929 people were still living in unsuitable places, as this report from a west London housing estate shows.

> Huts on the East Acton Estate are to be demolished and a block of flats is to be built in their place. The present tenants of the huts will be rehoused in the flats. The reason that flats are being erected instead of houses is that it is considered useless to move tenants from unsuitable buildings and then to offer them a house which would be much more expensive. (Quoted in the magazine of the *Oldoak Tenants' Association*, Acton, February 1929)

Why would it be considered useless to put tenants into more expensive accommodation? Do you agree with their argument?

A slum in the north of England in the early Twenties. Note the open drain in the middle of the street and the washtub hanging on the wall. The black object near the end of the street is a water pump. What does this tell you about the water supply to the houses?

## A HOME TO OURSELVES

Not everyone managed to get a council house, especially if they lived in the country. B.L. Coombes, who worked as a miner in South Wales, thought himself lucky to have a house where his family could live on their own.

> It was a small house; whitewashed; two small rooms downstairs and two up. No pantry and no scullery. The front door opened towards the main road and the other door opened directly into the kitchen. There was no passage, so if the front door was open at the same time as the back, we were lucky if we didn't have to buy a fresh lot of dishes to replace those blown off the dresser.
>
> Having no back entrance, the returning coal miner, and the coal when it came, had to be taken through the front room, in which my wife took such pride.
>
> The floor was below the level of the street and water ran down under the front door. In a wet winter we had water flowing in from the back. When I didn't step into water in the mornings I stepped onto black beetles, for there were thousands of them. . . . We could hear them at night, rustling as they moved over the papers; the pockets of my working clothes and often my boots were a favourite place with them.
>
> Despite its many drawbacks it was a house to ourselves, where we could talk without being overheard . . . besides, there was a small garden.

Notice there is no mention of a lavatory. This would probably have been at the end of the garden.

## TO THE SEASIDE

The coming of motor cars and buses allowed people, especially those who lived in rural areas, to travel further away from home and discover other parts of the country. Laurie Lee describes an outing in the Twenties by char-a-banc, a large open coach, from his Gloucestershire village to the seaside at Weston-Super-Mare.

> The first choir outing we ever had was a jaunt to Gloucester in a farm waggon. . . . Only the choir was included in that particular treat. Later, with the coming of the char-a-banc, the whole village took part as well. With the help of the powerful char-a-banc we got out of the district altogether; rattling away to the ends of the earth; to Bristol and even further afield. When the char-a-banc arrived everybody clambered aboard, fighting each other for seats. The char-a-banc was high, with open seats and folded tarpaulins at the rear on which the choir boys were privileged to sit. We all took our seats, people wrapped themselves in blankets, horns sounded, and we were ready to go.
>
> Mile after rattling mile we went under the racing sky. . . . The weather cleared as we drove into Weston and halted on the promenade. "The seaside", they said. (Laurie Lee, *Cider with Rosie*, 1959)

What do you think the tarpaulins were for? Find Gloucester and Bristol on the map at the back of the book. Are they very far apart? Why does Laurie Lee speak of them as "the ends of the earth"?

*Although Sainsbury's did make deliveries by motor they kept some of their horse-drawn vans, like this one which won a prize at a horse show.*

After the war motor lorries, vans, buses and private cars began to replace horse-drawn carriages and carts as forms of transport; this brought great changes to peoples' lives.

## PRIVATE CARS IN LONDON

By the mid-Twenties private cars were becoming cheaper and more people could afford them, but there were still not enough to cause serious traffic problems. This made driving, even in the big cities like London, easy.

> The first car I owned was a Morris Cowley. My father gave me a few driving lessons in his Buick, and when the day came for me to take delivery of my Morris Cowley I simply drove it away. In those days there were no driving tests, comparatively few private cars; no traffic wardens, parking meters or yellow lines near the curbs. Petrol was about 5p [1s.] a gallon. . . . You could park your car in London for hours at a time, in Bond Street or outside Harrods, but very few people left their cars out in the street at night. Everyone seemed to have some sort of garage. (C.V. Buckley, *Good Times at Home and Abroad*, 1979)

*These men from Yorkshire are out for a day trip. Char-a-banc outings became very popular in the early Twenties. Notice the old-fashioned motor horn on the front. What other things can you find which we no longer have on our cars or coaches?*

A Morris Cowley was a small, mass-produced car built at a place called Cowley, near Oxford. A Buick was a German car. Why, do you think, do we have many more regulations about driving now? Can you think of some regulations we have now which are not mentioned?

## NEW ROADS FOR OLD

Motor cars, buses and lorries needed wide, smooth roads on which to travel. This article from the *Wembley News*, January 1923, shows how the country lanes round Wembley were transformed to meet the needs of the Empire Exhibition in that year.

We have reached the end of Wembley's era of old-time country lane tranquility. With the march of Empire and, every day progress at Wembley, old-time peaceful country lanes are disappearing, and wider roads are being made for modern motor traffic.

One of these quiet old by-ways, Forty Lane, with its twelve-foot carriage way, is well on the way to being transformed into a sixty foot wide road. Neasden Lane, which will soon be equally wide, will be joined by the new North Way, one of the main roads from the North. This means that entirely new traffic, including omnibus traffic, will be created and visitors from north and west London can approach the Exhibition over wide roads.

## CAR TANK REPLENISHING MADE EASY

The coming summer is to see an ingenious system of motor spirit in bulk installed on all the main roads of the United Kingdom.... It takes the form of a standard pump outside the garage, drawing its supplies of petrol from a large underground reservoir. All the motorist has to do is to connect his car tank to the pump, by means of a flexible hose attached to the latter, then whatever quantity of petrol is required can be supplied. (*Hastings and St Leonards Observer*, 8 February 1921)

Before this, motorists had to carry cans of petrol with them. This was inconvenient and dangerous. Can you think why?

Does the person who wrote this really approve of the coming of these new highways? Do you think he was right to regret the passing of the old-time peaceful tranquility of Wembley?

# The Suburbs

There was no room inside the large towns and cities to build all the houses that were needed after the war, but the coming of the motor car and the bus and the extension of public transport made it possible for people to live in one place and work in another, travelling every day from their homes to their office or factory. This was to change the way of life of many people and to change the face of the countryside.

## A LONDON COUNTY COUNCIL HOUSING ESTATE

After the war the London Transport underground railway was extended from the centre of the city into the countryside to the north and west. When the underground reached Edgware, north of the capital, the LCC began building a large estate, called Watling, to house the thousands of London people who needed somewhere to live. The first houses were opened in 1926, but for several years life on the estate was difficult, as this account by a man who went there as an eight-year-old boy shows.

**I have known the Watling estate from the early days when buttercups were still growing at the place where there are now big shops, in Watling Avenue.**

**Mud was in the streets; there were no shops then and no schools; the children were running wild. Only part of the estate stood, and only houses had been built. At that time there was nothing but bricks and mortar and acres of mud. If one wanted to dance, or attend a concert, one had to travel into London or to one of the pubs, some distance away.** (The Watling Residents' Association, *Reminiscences of a Watling Resident*, 1934)

Within a few years shops, cinemas and schools had come to Watling and the people were living in better conditions than most of them had ever had in London.

These houses, built along the side of the roads like this, gave homes to many people but what did they do to the countryside? Stanley Baldwin, the Prime Minister, said: "In fifty years' time, at the rate at which these improvements are being made, the destruction of all the beauty and charm of our towns and villages will be complete." Do you think he was right? Can you find out what has been done to prevent this from happening?

## THE RUSH-HOUR

As the number of families living on the Watling estate grew, travelling on the underground trains became more and more difficult, as Ruth Durant recounts:

**Now that the district is getting more and more thickly populated, from 7 a.m. to the last workmen's train at 7.30 a.m. there is a continuous flow of people to the station. At one time one booking clerk, working at top speed, could just manage to issue the necessary tickets during the rush-hour. Now there are three clerks, and three lines of people queued up to buy tickets. Most of the regulars take up a position on the platform where they know the door will open when the train stops. Sometimes the train pulls up short, and then there is a rush for the doors. Those who get a seat are lucky.**
(Reminiscences of a Watling Resident, 1937)

If you have ever travelled on the London underground in the rush hour you will know that it is still like that today. What other cities in Britain have underground railways?

Private builders as well as the local councils were building houses on the outskirts of London, as this advertisement shows.

**The estate is most attractive, on a beautiful slope only twelve miles from London.
The situation is magnificent, over 400 feet above sea level with wonderful views in all directions.
The estate is charmingly wooded with avenues of trees, a spinney and woods which are very delightful.
The houses have two or three reception rooms, four bedrooms, a tiled bathroom, a kitchen and all the usual offices.
The houses are labour-saving and easily worked. Electric light and heat, gas, main drainage, company water supply and telephone are all available.
The smallest garden is nearly half an acre, giving ample space for tennis courts, kitchen garden and flower garden.
The train service from London – Baker Street or Marylebone – is excellent.
The journey takes only twenty minutes and there are forty trains a day.
THE PRICE £1,595 freehold. The County Garden Estates Ltd.**
(From *Ideal Home*, December 1924)

What items listed here make you think these houses would have been for the relatively well-off? Compare this advertisement with the kind of estate agents' details issued today.

*As more housing was made available in the suburbs the London Underground extended its network to bring the workers into the city centre. Hendon Central Station was opened in 1924. See if you can find Hendon on a modern London Underground map.*

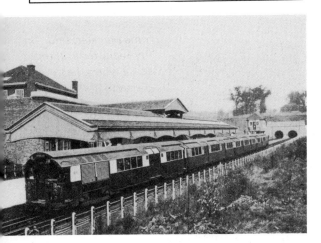

# New Technology in the Home

## COUNTRY HOUSE LIGHTING

This advertisement from the magazine *Ideal Home* July 1924 appeals to someone who is thinking of "going electric".

**What do you expect from electricity?**
**Is it to light ten rooms or twenty?**
**What about electric fires?**
**Will the maids use electric irons?**
**Are you thinking of a vacuum cleaner?**

**You probably have a good idea as to what you want but perhaps you are not sure as to whether your wishes are reasonably possible.**

What sort of doubts do you think people might have about introducing electricity into their homes?

## THE DAILY MAIL IDEAL LABOUR-SAVING HOME

In 1924 the Daily Mail ran a competition, with a first prize of £500, to find the "Ideal Labour-Saving Home". The winning design had the following labour-saving points:

**One servant**
**No open fires**
**No carrying water to bedrooms**
**No space wasted on passages**
**Central heating and electric fires**
**Soiled linen shutes from kitchen to outside bin**
**No bright surface to be polished**
**No square corners to attract dust.**

Some of these things are common in houses today, but in 1924 they would have been beyond the reach of most ordinary people.

After the war, when high taxation forced even wealthy people to cut costs and there was a shortage of domestic servants, new houses were designed to make it easier to run them without much help. The extension of gas and electricity to many more homes made it possible to introduce labour-saving gadgets which transformed many people's lifestyles.

## NO VACUUM CLEANERS

When a large house was not wired for electricity or labour-saving devices, work for the housemaids was still very hard, as Lavinia Swinbrook recalls. She started work in 1925 at the age of 14 for a family of three.

**There were no vacuum cleaners, so carpets had to brushed with a small hard brush, with either salt or tea leaves to settle the dust. In a kneeling position, of course. There were awful open grates with steel fire-irons, thicker than my skinny arms, to be polished every day; the glass screens over the grates to be washed with a wash leather; and finally, the basin of whitening powder to be carried from room to room.**

All this to be done in time for breakfast, as her time-table shows.

**Timetable**
6.30 a.m.  **Rise.**
**Clean grate and lay fire in dining room. Sweep and dust. Clean grate and lay fire in billiard room. Sweep and dust.**
**Polish the staircase.**

## DIFFICULTIES IN WIRING AN OLD HOUSE

It was not always easy to wire an old house for electricity, as this entry for June 1922 in the diary of Sir Henry Rider Haggard shows.

> **The house is upside down and filled with men who are putting in electric light. . . . It is not easy to wire a solid brick house that is full of oak panelling and parquet floors but we could no longer bear the darkness of this house, especially now as there is no one to do the oil lamps, of which we had such a number in the old days.**

This extract shows some of the difficulties caused by the shortage of "living-in" domestic servants after the war. Daily cleaning women were not there when the fires needed to be lit.

We take for granted all the things in this advertisement for electric appliances, but to the young housewife in the Twenties they were quite new and very exciting.

|          | Clean grate and lay fire in morning room. |
|----------|-------------------------------------------|
|          | Clean grate and lay fire in drawing room. |
|          | Sweep and dust the vestibule. |
|          | Sweep and dust blue staircase. |
|          | [All before breakfast.] |
| 8 a.m.   | Breakfast in the servants' hall. |
| 9 a.m.   | Start bedrooms. Help with bed making and slops and fill carafes. |
|          | Clean grates and lay fires, fill up coal boxes and wood baskets. |
|          | Sweep and dust bedrooms. |
|          | Change into afternoon clothes. |
| 1 p.m.   | Lunch in servants' hall. |

| Afternoons | Clean silver, brass water-cans. Trim lamps. |
|------------|---------------------------------------------|
| 4 p.m.     | Tea in servants' hall. |
| 5 p.m.     | Light fires in bedrooms. |
| 6 p.m.     | Cans of hot water to bedrooms. |
| 7.30 p.m.  | Turn down beds, make up fires, fill up coal boxes. |

(Quoted in John Burnett, ed., *Useful Toil: Autobiographies of Working People from 1820s to 1920s*, 1974)

Compare this with the new labour-saving home.

# Changes in the Village

After the war, as machines began to take over from horses on the farm and new forms of transport linked the countryside to the town, the old pattern of village life began to change.

## THE DISAPPEARANCE OF SMALL WORKSHOPS

The Chief Inspector of Factories and Workshops in his report for the year 1927 claimed:

**There is evidence of the decline of the small country establishments; the saddler and the blacksmith, the village tailor and the milliner are all steadily going out of business. This decline is most apparent in East Anglia and the rural areas of Wales, but even in London the smaller employers are finding great difficulty in competing with larger establishments.**

Can you think of any reason in particular why blacksmiths and saddlers were going out of business at this time?

*Workmen repairing the thatch on an old cottage in a small village in Worcestershire.*

## SHOPS AND SERVICES IN THE VILLAGE

Even in 1927 some villages still maintained a fairly wide range of services and shops as this table from Ringmer in Sussex shows:

| Publicans | 5 | Wheelwright | 1 | Tax collector | 1 |
|---|---|---|---|---|---|
| Boot & | | Grocers | 3 | Laundry | 1 |
| Shoemakers | 2 | Builders | 2 | Undertaker | 1 |
| Carpenters | 1 | Insurance | | Blacksmiths | 1 |
| Cornmiller | 1 | agent | 1 | Garage | 1 |
| Barbers | 2 | Chimney | | | |
| | | sweep | 1 | | |

(*Kelly's Directory for Sussex*, 1927)

*These boys are trying to decide how to spend their ▷ pennies at the village shop. You could get quite a lot of sweets for a penny. Notice the old fashioned sweet jars in the window.*

If there is a village near you try to find out how many of these shops and services can be found today. Can you think of any one of these which has increased?

## SLATE ROOFS

New houses being built in the village at this time were not always welcome, as this letter to *Country Life* magazine, published on the 26 April 1924, shows:

> The village is small and old and any new buildings immediately attract attention. . . . For several weeks now two small cottages are being erected at the end of the chief street and yesterday they began to put on the roofs. They are actually using slates.
>
> Now the traveller will walk up the village street past a row of white walled thatched cottages when he will suddenly be confronted by the uninspiring grey of new slates. Surely there is enough red brick and dirty grey slate in our towns without it being necessary to tamper with what few untouched villages remain. . . . When the invasion is complete we shall perhaps be able to see an example of real thatch in our museums.

Why, do you think, were the new roofs made of slate rather than thatch? What advantages does slate have over thatch?

## ELECTRICITY COMES TO THE VILLAGE

Many villages were slow in getting electricity and not everyone was happy about it when it did come, as Edward Short recalls:

> The first stage of our village electrification came when the saw-mill changed hands. . . . Tommy Taylor was an electricity enthusiast who quickly extended the system through the village. That was when we parted company with our oil lamps and candles. When it was switched on my father insisted on comparing the two brass lamps which hung from a beam in the middle of the living room against the single electric bulb which hung alongside them. He was in no doubt which gave the better light: the oil lamps. He was probably right, but the convenience of being able to switch the light on and off at the wall was too great and in the end he was won over; though at 10d. a unit we had to switch off when there was nobody in the room. (Edward Short, *I Knew My Place*, 1983)

# The Stately Homes of England

Before the war the most important person in the village was often the squire. He was wealthy, lived in a very large house, often filled with valuable pictures and furniture, and owned a great deal of land. He belonged to a different class from the people of the village.

Because of high taxation many of these landowners were not quite so wealthy after the war, and if their sons had been killed in the conflict and there was no direct heir the land might be sold and the family move away.

## WE FELL APART

In *Cider with Rosie* (published in 1959) Laurie Lee describes what happened in his village in Gloucestershire when the old squire died and his nephew decided to sell up.

> **The Big House was sold by auction and became a home for invalids. The lake silted up, the swans flew away, and the great pike choked in the reeds. With the squire's hand removed, we (the villagers) fell apart. . . . His servants dispersed and went into factories. . .**

Why do you think the village "fell apart" when the squire died?

## LAND SALES

Not all landowners sold up their houses and left the village. Many of them continued to live in their splendid country houses, but they sold part of their land to help to keep them going. This account of a coming land sale was the first of many that appeared in the newspapers between 1920 and 1921.

## IN THE SERVICE OF A GENTLEMAN

Though their estates might be smaller, life in a country house could still be quite comfortable as Lavinia Swinbank, who went to one in 1927 as a servant, was to discover.

> **My next position was in the stately home of a titled lady and gentleman and here I really learned for the the first time the meaning of "gentleman's service". For the first time I was treated like a human being by people with heart and consideration for all their staff. We were even given the unheard of privilege of two hours off in the afternoon. . .**

> **The first of the year's land sales takes place at Bristol on Jan 6th when outlying parts of the Duke of Badminton's estates in Gloucestershire and Wiltshire are offered for sale. Extending over 4,000 acres . . . in addition to small-holdings there are a dozen good grazing and dairy farms, all situated on hard roads.** (The *Daily Telegraph*, 5 January 1920)

The Duke of Beaufort still owns a splendid house at Badminton in Wiltshire. Can you think of an annual event which takes place there and is shown on television?

Is there a country house near you? Find out all you can about it. Who owns it? Is it open to visitors? Find out, too, about the National Trust, which helps to preserve these stately homes for us to enjoy, if the owners cannot afford to keep them.

When the family returned from the Season in London with the young members of the family and their friends ("The Bright Young Things", they were called) house parties were frequent. To me it was exciting to see how the other half lived. I used to watch over the bannisters, the young people in their wonderful dresses dancing to the strains of the gramophone in the brightly lit hall. (Quoted in John Burnett, ed., *Useful Toil*, 1974)

## MAKING LAND MORE PROFITABLE

Sometimes when a large estate changed hands the new owner was able to introduce new farming methods or new breeds of cattle which helped to make the land more profitable. Here is an account of what was done on a large estate in Surrey when it had been taken over by a new owner from Ireland. It also tells us something of the life still lived by a wealthy landowner.

Captain R.E. Palmer owns some of the best pure bred Kerry [cattle] that are to be found in, or outside, Ireland. The Captain is a prominent member of the local district council. . . . He is a genial man, loved by all his tenants. A typical sportsman in the hunting field, racing circles, yachting and with rod and gun. . . . Some fine specimens of his skill as an angler together with relics of his big game hunting are to be seen at Oaklands. . .

The accommodation for his cattle is all that could be looked for. The sheds and byres are kept clean and healthy. The first electric light to be installed in this district was in his sheds and pig styes. (From an article in The *Countryside Review*, 22 December, 1924)

What do you think the relics of big game hunting might have been? Where would Captain Palmer have been to collect them? Make a list of the different sports in which Captain Palmer was interested. How can you tell from this that he was a wealthy man?

*For the Bright Young Things, the sons and daughters of wealthy landowners, life was one long party: house parties in the country were popular and, during the Season, so were wild, extravagant parties at fashionable London hotels. The carnival pictured here is on the roof garden of the Criterion hotel. The guests are having a snow-ball fight with cotton wool balls!*

# Clothes and Manners

The Great War brought many changes in the way young people lived. Manners were much less formal, clothes were more casual, and young people were more free to live their own lives away from their parents. Those who could afford it drove fast cars. Girls shortened their skirts and cut their hair. Young men and women smoked cigarettes and drank cocktails.

## NEW FASHIONS

Wearing make-up, short skirts and bobbed hair began amongst the Bright Young Things, whose homes were the stately mansions and whose photographs appeared in the newspapers, but they were soon being worn in a cheaper form, by girls who lived a very different life. Winifred Foley, who came to London at the age of 14 to work as a servant, found this out when she met Blodwen, another maid with whom she was to work.

> **She [Blodwen] didn't look like my idea of a maid at all. Her good looks were hidden under an overdose of lipstick, rouge and mascara. She had the first cropped hair I had ever seen and she wore a flapper length black satin coat fastened with one fancy button. She wore high heeled black court shoes and pink silk stockings. I was most impressed.** (Winifred Foley, *A Child in the Forest*, 1974)

A "flapper" was a young woman who liked to wear unusual clothes and shock her parents and their friends by her daring behaviour. Blodwen was off-duty when Winifred met her. When she was working she wore a maid's cap and apron.

*Blodwen might have looked something like this, though without the large fur collar, when Winifred Foley met her.*

## HOUSE PARTIES

C.V. Buckley, a wealthy young man who had been to Eton, was a regular guest at house parties. He explains why he was invited and why he enjoyed them.

> **When I worked in a London shipping office in the 1920s I first began to enjoy invitations to country house parties. I had a car, played tennis, could dance the Charleston, and I got my suits from Saville Row. My portable gramophone records were mostly sent from America; an unheard-of luxury.**

Smart Coat in chi...
finished velveteen,
on most attractive li...
with new flared sk...
finished handsome co...
and cuffs of good qua...
fur, and lined throu...
out with crêpe de chi...
In black and ni...
brown only. Stoc...
in three sizes

Price **10** gns.

Sent on Approval

Debenham &
Freebod...
Wigmore Stre...
London W...

The Prince of Wales (third from the left) at the Royal and Ancient Golf Club at St Andrews in Scotland. The Prince is wearing plus-fours, which he helped to make fashionable.

A house with a large domestic staff, grass and hard tennis courts, and with a nearby golf course made it easy for hosts to entertain weekend guests. The men wore plus-fours, Oxford bags and, in the evening, double-breasted dinner jackets that had just come into fashion after the Prince of Wales started wearing them.

Plus-fours were loose baggy trousers, gathered into a band below the knee. Oxford bags were trousers that flared round the ankles. Saville Row is a street in London's fashionable Mayfair, where men's suits are still tailor-made. The Charleston and the Tango were the two most popular dances when the dance craze swept over England. Like the jazz music which accompanied them, they were imported from the United States.

## THE DANCING CRAZE

The Bright Young Things were not the only ones to enjoy dancing in the 1920s. A craze for dancing swept the whole country and dance halls grew up all over the place. Robert Roberts, a young man living in Salford, a working-class district of Lancashire, describes how he and his friends went dancing:

Some of us went jigging as often as six times a week. The great barn we went to held at least a thousand. Almost every day it was jammed with masses of young men and women of all classes, mixing for the first time. For sixpence a time ... youths and girls of every level of the working class foxtrotted through the new bliss in each others' arms ... "Momma goes here" we sang "Momma goes there, Momma goes jazzing everywhere". (Robert Roberts, The Classic Slum, 1974)

## ONLY FOR THE GENTRY

Few people in the Cumbrian village of Warcop would have been affected by the new fashion in men's clothes. Plus-fours and Oxford bags were only for the gentry, but, as Edward Short explains, there was a rigid demarcation between Sunday clothes and weekday clothes, except for the gentry: they wore Sunday clothes all the time.

Almost all the men wore blue serge suits [on Sunday] with narrow trousers that finished a couple of inches above their boots. Low shoes were avant-garde, and therefore only for the gentry. I never had a proper suit as a young boy. It was always short trousers (breeches, we called them), grey jerseys and long grey stockings with coloured rings round the top, which I could never keep up. No boy got long trousers until he reached the age of fourteen or fifteen and then he was so self-conscious that he had to be pushed into going to church. (Edward Short, I Knew My Place, 1983)

# Women at Work

Not all young women wanted to shock their parents or go dancing every night. Some went to college or trained for a career, but it was not easy. During the war women had been allowed to do all kinds of new jobs, but when the men came home many women had to give up their jobs and go on the dole. However, there were more opportunities in the Twenties for women, even if they had to fight hard to be allowed to take them up. For the first time women were allowed to vote in elections and become Members of Parliament. Some became civil servants and lawyers.

## UNEMPLOYMENT WAS BAD

1921 was a bad year for unemployment. Bessie Ward, an 18-year-old who lived in Middlesex, describes her experiences at that time.

> I first met Mr Smith in 1921. He had just started this new business in Cricklewood, in an old disused stable. He had one girl, near my own age, working for him. . . . The labour exchange sent me to Mr Smith as he was about to open his first factory for potato crisp production. I was forced to take the position of packing crisps or lose my dole, as it was called. It was a job I hated as we had forms with no backs to rest against and my finger tips were torn to pieces. We tried wearing gloves but they were in holes in no time. The chips used to be served up in large . . . baths with a girl sitting on each side. We were on piecework and were paid so much for a tray, but we were lucky if we earned fifteen shillings a week. . . (From a letter written by Bessie Ward to Smiths Potato Crisp Company in 1982 when she was nearly 80 years old)

Mr Smith's business flourished. In 1928 one million packets of his potato crisps were sold.

## DELIVERING THE BREAD

During the war women drove ambulances and even buses, and after the war a few wealthy ones drove their own cars, but not many of them were driving a baker's van before they were 20, like this girl from St Helens in Lancashire.

> I joined the bakery at fifteen when I left school. Leonard Swift was well known then. His son taught me to drive. It was a T type Ford van. . . . You had to start it by hand. . . . I was 17 when I started delivering. . . . You hardly met any other traffic. You could go for miles over cobbled streets and round corners without being afraid of bumping into anything. The only rule of the road was to keep on the left side. . . . You got seventeen shillings, with all the responsibility of driving the van. You worked all hours. At Christmas I used to be out until two o'clock on Christmas morning. I took parcels and turkeys. I used to be jiggered for Christmas – I spent most of it in bed. (Quoted in C. Foreman, *Industrial Town: Self Portrait of St Helens in the 1920s*, 1979)

At that time cars and vans were started by inserting a handle under the bonnet and turning it until the engine sprang into life.

Find out where your bread comes from. Is it baked locally? Does the baker still deliver bread to the door?

Amy Johnson waves to the crowd at Croydon Airport after a return flight from South Africa to London. She undertook this after the flight to Australia which made her famous.

## THE ROAD TO SUCCESS FOR WOMEN

Amy Johnson, after studying at University College, Sheffield, took a job in a London office to earn enough money to take flying lessons. She was determined to fly and eventually qualified as a pilot in 1929. Writing about the difficulties she had encountered Amy said:

> **For a man, training for a career in aviation is easy and cheap, and jobs are numerous and well paid at the end of it. A man . . . can join the Royal Air Force. . . he can become an airline pilot, an instructor, a navigator, a radio operator or a record-breaker. For a woman there is not the same opportunity. The RAF is closed to her and there is too much prejudice to allow her a job like an airline pilot. She may however, have the chance of being . . . an air taxi pilot, and there are odd jobs like trailing advertisement banners for which she may be accepted.**
> **. . . For a woman the road to success is not well sign-posted with cut and dried methods of training, and regular jobs and regular pay at the end of it. There is still prejudice to be overcome.** (Amy Johnson, *Sky Roads of the World*, 1939)

## THEY CHOSE FREEDOM

After the war many girls were reluctant to go into domestic service. They preferred almost anything else which would give them more free time.

> **The independent teenage girl of the poor working class is flatly rejecting any kind of domestic service. English working class girls now prefer any sort of job in a mill or factory, or even a job with rock bottom wages at Woolworths with their freedom, rather than the best that domestic service can offer them.**
> (Quoted in Robert Roberts, *The Classic Slum*, 1974)

Why do you think that girls were refusing to go into service? What effect would the fall in numbers of domestic staff have had on the households of the well-to-do?

Amy Johnson never became a regular airline pilot, but she did become a record-breaker when she flew to Australia, single-handed, in 1930. Try to find out more about her career. Are there any women airline pilots today?

# In the Air

Aeroplanes were flying before 1914 and were used for military purposes by both sides during the war. In 1919 a regular air service to Paris was set up, carrying mail and a few passengers, but flying as a new form of travel was slow to develop beyond this.

## LONDON TO PARIS, 1920

C.V. Buckley, who left school in 1920, describes his flight on one of these cross-Channel routes.

> In 1920 I persuaded my father to take me on one of the first commercial flights to Paris from Croydon. Our craft was a converted Avro reconnaissance war plane . . . the one-way fare was £25. We took off from a grass runway. There were only two seats for passengers. The pilot sat outside in the cockpit. Speaking through an intercom telephone he told us that we would be flying at 4,000 feet and that, all being well, we would land at Paris airport . . . in two and a half-hours. At 60 m.p.h. we made the trip in two hours, and good visibility made it possible for us to see the war-devastated parts of France: trenches, shell craters, abandoned tanks and gun emplacements . . . (C.V. Buckley, *Good Times at Home and Abroad*, 1979)

Find out how long it takes to fly from London to Paris now. Do you think £25 is a lot for the one-way fare (remember that petrol cost about 1s. [5p] a gallon and it cost about 6d [less than 3p] to go to the cinema in the Twenties)?

## ON THE THRESHOLD OF A NEW AGE

At the Empire Exhibition at Wembley in 1924, British aeroplanes were on display and took part in a military tattoo. Sir Philip Sassoon, the Secretary of State for Air, sent the following message to the Wembley Exhibition.

> To no nation does flying mean more than to the widely scattered people of the British Empire. No nation has a greater need of better communications. Sea communications made possible the foundation of the British Empire. Air communications will make possible . . . its full development. Look forward to the progress which can now be counted on with confidence. We are on the threshold of a new age, let us take and keep a lead in it.

Why would air communications have been so important to the British Empire?

## WESTMINSTER VIA AUSTRALIA

Despite the brave efforts of flyers, both men and women, who flew alone across oceans and continents to show what could be done, there was no great interest in developing flying as a means of travel. Alan Cobham, who had flown to South Africa and back, said on the radio:

> This flight was not a stunt; none of my flights were stunts. The idea was a flight to survey right across the African continent and back again so that I could make a report of all the difficulties, landing grounds, climate, the possibility of flying through monsoons, etc.

△
After the War both the British and the Germans believed that the future of air travel was with the huge gas filled airships sometimes known as Zeppelins (after the German inventor). The passengers travelled in a cabin slung under the body of the airship. This picture shows the British ship the R101 leaving her mooring tower in 1929. The following year on her first flight to India she crashed in flames in France, killing all but six of her 54 passengers, including the Minister for Air. Britain built no more airships after that. The future belonged to the aeroplane, after all.

Alan Cobham standing in front of his plane, a DH50, after competing for the King's Cup in 1924, one year before he made his famous flight to Cape Town and back.
▽

I got to the Cape and back but even I could not wake the government up to the fact that we could start airlines all over the world. Nobody in Parliament wanted to know. I remember talking to an official from the Air Ministry who said, "Cobham, what you ought to do is to fly a seaplane from Rochester and land in front of the Houses of Parliament; that would wake them up." I said, "That's a good idea, but I'll tell you what I'll do: I'll take off from the Medway and land in front of the Houses of Parliament, but I will do it via Australia." (Quoted in Lesley Baily and C.H. Brewer, eds., *BBC Scrapbook for 1925*, 1937)

Two years later Alan Cobham flew a plane to Australia and back, a distance of 26,000 miles, and landed outside the Houses of Parliament. He was knighted for this trip.

Can you think of any reasons why air travel did not develop very fast? What do you think many people might feel about flying in the air?

29

# On the Air

The first radio message had been transmitted across the Atlantic in 1903 and radio communications had been used during the war, but it was in the Twenties that wireless was able to reach the homes of ordinary people. The British Broadcasting Corporation was set up in 1922 and millions of people were able to hear reports of national events and listen to concerts in their own homes.

*An early wireless set from Gamages, a famous ▷ London store. Note the earphones. Many people thought the coming of the wireless one of the most important innovations of the Twenties. Can you think of the ways in which it must have changed people's lives?*

### THE FIRST WIRELESS CONCERT

The first wireless concert was given by Dame Nellie Melba, the famous singer, on 16 June 1920. The concert was sponsored by the *Daily Mail* newspaper. Tom Clarke, a journalist on the paper, wrote in his diary:

> We had the Melba concert last night. She went to the Marconi works in Chelmsford. Soon after seven o'clock she started singing into a microphone. I listened in at Blackfriars in London. There were not enough aerials so we listened in turn. Melba's secretary was there; her eyes nearly popped out of her head as she heard the nightingale voice: "It is Melba", she cried in astonishment.
>
> Today we are receiving messages from all parts of the world. All Europe was her audience last night. Messages from liners at sea tell us that the passengers listened to Melba, far across the water. (Tom Clarke, *My Life with Lord Northcliffe*, 17 June 1920)

THIS is the most advanced Crystal Set yet produced, and without equal for reception within 25 miles from the Broadcasting Station.

Gam
WIRE
CATAL
will interest
us send you a

**POINTS OF SUPERIORITY**

1
*Extremely wide range of tuning, enabling interruptions to be cut out.*

2
*Dust-proof detector keeps crystal sensitive for a very long period.*

3
*The buzzer helps you to find sensitive spot on crystal quickly, and before the broadcasting begins.*

4
*Perfect undistorted reception, and powerful enough to take SIX PAIRS of phones under normal condition.*

5
*The only upkeep cost is the occasional replacement of crystal—the famous "Gamage Permanite," price 1/6 per piece.*

6
*Terminals are provided for addition of extra inductance to increase the wave-length. Thus you can receive the Paris Time Signals and the like.*

7
*We want to prove to you that this set is unrivalled. Call at Holborn and test it for yourself—free of charge—during Broadcasting hours.*

# GAMAGE
## "IDEAL" CRYST
## RECEIVING S

FULLY licensed by Postmaster-General and stamped Regd. No. 226. Tuning Coil wound with best quality tapped in seven places. This, when used in conjunction Variable Condenser, which is of the best possible workmansh good variation of tuning. The Crystal Detector, designed dust from deteriorating the sensitivity of the crystal, contains "Permanite" Crystal, which has given such excellent results. Condenser is incorporated, while terminals are fitted for extra High-grade, sensitive Headphones are supplied. The task of sensitive spot on the crystal is minimised by means of a bu receive telephony for 25 miles, and signals from Spark statio wave length of 300-500 metres for 450 to 700 miles. Complete Mahogany Cabinet, with instruments mounted on polished 'Phones, Aerial Wire, and Insulators ready for use.   Price

# £4 4s.

CRYSTAL RECEIVER only, without 'Phones   £2
or Aerial Accessories                        Price

—— *Carriage Paid.* ——

## A. W. GAMAGE, L
## HOLBORN, LONDON, I

### I CAN SEE YOU

Although television was not shown until the Thirties, and did not become a national network until after the Second World War, the first TV picture was produced as early as 1925 by an inventor, John Logie Baird. William Taynton, whose face first appeared on the screen, explained what happened.

> Baird called me upstairs to his office where I saw a strange contraption. . . . He asked me to sit down in front of the

POST OFFICE TELEPHONES

COVER THE COUNTRY

NO INSTALLATION CHARGE
SMALL QUARTERLY RENTAL.

*An advertisement for telephones issued by The Post Office. Since the end of the First World War the telephone had been taking over, as a way of sending messages, from the telegraph. By January 1927 Europe and the USA were connected by lines across the Atlantic.*

machine. . . . Mr Baird then went into the next room. Several very powerful lights were nearly touching my face . . . the heat was terrific . . . I could stand no more than a minute of it. I pulled back but Mr Baird shouted "Hang on a second longer; put out your tongue, shake your head, open your eyes." All the time I was getting baked alive. Then he yelled "I can see you; William, I can see you."
(Quoted in Leslie Baily and C.H. Brewer, eds., *BBC Scrapbook for 1925*, 1937)

## WEEKEND RADIO PROGRAMME

For Saturday, 29 January 1929.

**Daily religious service
Weather report
Rugby International
The Carlton Sextet dance band
Children's Hour
News bulletin.**

Compare this with the radio programmes listed in today's *Radio Times*. Make a list of all the different kinds of programmes you can listen to today.

## THE VERY WORD WAS MAGIC TO ME

Wireless sets were expensive to buy in the early days, but it was not difficult to build a set for yourself, as Edward Short, a teenager at the time, tells us:

**In my teens I became passionately absorbed with the greatest miracle of the post-war world: the wireless. The very word was magic to me. . . . I kept every written word I could find about it, and spent all the money I earned, by delivering fish, on mysterious crystals, cats' whiskers, earcoils and all the other ingredients of this modern wonder.**

**When a new magazine called *Modern Wireless* came out in 1922, I read it from cover to cover until it ceased publication . . . and I made my first crystal, one valve set and three valve sets from the plans they published.**
(Edward Short, *I Know My Place*, 1983)

# Empire Matters

## EMPIRE DAY

Dorothy Gulliver, in an interview made specially for this book, recalls that at her primary school in north London:

> **Empire Day was celebrated each year to remind us of all the different countries which were part of the British Empire and of the people of different colours and religions who, like us, had George V as their king. We had a special morning assembly; everyone brought a little Union Jack flag, and those who really did come from one of the other Empire countries were asked to stand on the stage wearing their national costume. In the centre sat Britannia, a girl chosen because of her red hair and good behaviour to wear the armour and hold the trident, just like the figure on the penny coin. Other children were chosen to represent children from other lands; an Indian girl, wearing a sari, perhaps. . . . At the back of the stage was hung a big map of the world with all the British countries coloured red, and with the words "The empire on which the sun never sets". The headmistress read a message to the schools from the King and we sang patriotic hymns. After "God save the King", the dressed-up children led us out into the playground and we all marched past Britannia and saluted a large Union Jack she was holding. The rest of the day was a holiday.**

Britain no longer talks about her empire but most of the countries which were once part of it still have a special link with her. Can you find out what it is? Make a list of all the countries you know which have this link.

Over the centuries Britain had built up a great overseas empire and, in the difficult years after the war, trade with these colonies became very important. To help the British people to take a pride in their overseas possessions and to encourage trade, 24 May was set aside every year as Empire Day, to be observed with parades, articles in the newspapers, and with special ceremonies in schools.

## I LIKE AUSTRALIA IMMENSELY

In the Twenties many young people who were dissatisfied in this country and could find no work left to start a new life in one of the Empire countries, particularly Australia, Canada or New Zealand. In March 1927 the magazine *Emigration* carried this account from a 19-year-old girl from Sussex, who had gone to Australia in the autumn of 1925 to find work.

> **I arrived here on November 27th. . . . I find Australia an open and free country to anyone who is willing to work. . . . I myself did domestic work in England and am doing the same in Sydney. I regard the principal differences between here and England as follows:**
>
> **A young domestic help will find she gets more freedom here.**
> **She will get more money and work less hours.**
> **She will find the houses smaller and easy to work**
> **The English girl will find the Australian mistress very kind.**
> **I myself am working at a hospital; I only work eight hours a day with three hours' rest in between.**

## ALL SORTS OF STRANGE AND WONDERFUL THINGS

Most people who went to the Empire Exhibition at Wembley were excited by it, particularly if they watched the Pageant of Empire or the military displays. But this report from an overseas visitor is rather different. He was a merchant seaman from Somaliland in East Africa, who travelled the world on a cargo boat and was staying in London at the time.

> **My friend told me of a place called Wembley where things from many parts of the world were to be seen; and we went there together. Here we saw big machines moving by themselves and all sorts of strange and wonderful things. I felt overwhelmed by it all. It appeared to me as if the world had been made for Europeans who had only to stretch out their hands to bring before them, as if by magic, all the products of universe.** (From Richard Pankhurst, ed., *An Early Somali Autobiography*, 1977)

Do you think the seaman was impressed by what he saw? Do you think he minded that "it appeared as if the world had been made for Europeans"?

> **I am earning 35 shillings a week and all my keep.**
> **I have one and a half days off a week and every evening from 6.30 p.m.**
> **I can come in at any time I like as long as I am on duty at 6.30 next morning.**
>
> **So, I am quite happy and like Australia immensely.**

Compare her working day with that of Lavinia Swinbank described on page 18.

BRITISH EMPIRE EXHIBITION 1924

WEMBLEY · LONDON

APRIL – OCTOBER

REGISTERED OFFICES:
14-16 GROSVENOR GARDENS
LONDON, S.W. 1

TELEGRAMS · "IMPERIUM, SOWEST, LONDON"
TELEPHONES · · · · VICTORIA 8860-1-2

ADMISSION 1'6 CHILDREN HALF PRICE

On 23 April 1924 King George V opened a great Empire Exhibition at Wembley, where products and displays from all the countries of the Empire were exhibited to the public in specially built halls and pavilions. The exhibition, which continued into a second year, was a great success.

# The Health of the Nation

There was no National Health Service in the Twenties, so the range of medical services open to people was limited, although the National Insurance Act of 1920 gave some help with the cost of doctors' bills and medicines to employed people. Outside the areas of high unemployment – the north of England, Scotland and Wales – nourishing food, better housing and a slightly higher living standard generally meant better health for the people of Britain.

## THE COST OF BEING ILL

The Ministry of Health, set up in 1919, did much to improve the health of children by a system of school inspections. Marjorie Martin, who lived at Hastings, remembers:

> I had German measles once and my mother surmised it was German measles, but she thought she ought to call in the doctor, and it cost her half a crown, just for telling her what she already knew. I felt dreadful at costing my mother half a crown.
> When I was young I was suspected of being tubercular. I had to have a glass of milk every day at school. A nurse came round and they had doctors there. I was the one who was not going to live beyond seven years, so the doctor told my mother, and yet I don't remember being ill except for the German measles.... (Quoted in *Hastings Voices*, 1937)

## DIPHTHERIA

Scarlet fever and diphtheria were two diseases common among children in the Twenties. They were very infectious and patients had to be moved to special isolation hospitals away from everyone else. A joiner from St Helens recalls what other treatment was given.

## SCHOOL MEALS

Providing meals at school for children in need had begun before the war, but the growing concern for the health and welfare of children, particularly in areas of high unemployment, led to an increase in the number of school meals being served. Dr G.F. Buchanan, the Medical Officer of Health for Willesden, in his report of September 1920 showed how important school dinners could be to some children.

> Children seem to be quickly improved physically. They seem more vigorous and alert and lose the apathetic, interest-lacking expression characteristic of children from poor homes. It is noticeable that where a varied diet and abundance of food is given, as at the Education Committee centre, there are nothing like so many children suffering from sores.

> When people had diphtheria someone used to come and disinfect your house. Every room would be sealed and men from the town hall would pump gas into the place to kill off the infection. They used to bathe the people in eucalyptus oil; you could tell for weeks after when they had been in hospital. (Quoted in C.F. Forman, ed., *Industrial Town: Self Portrait of St Helens in the 1920s*, 1979)

How could you tell for weeks after that they had been in hospital? Diphtheria and scarlet fever are no longer a problem. Can you think why?

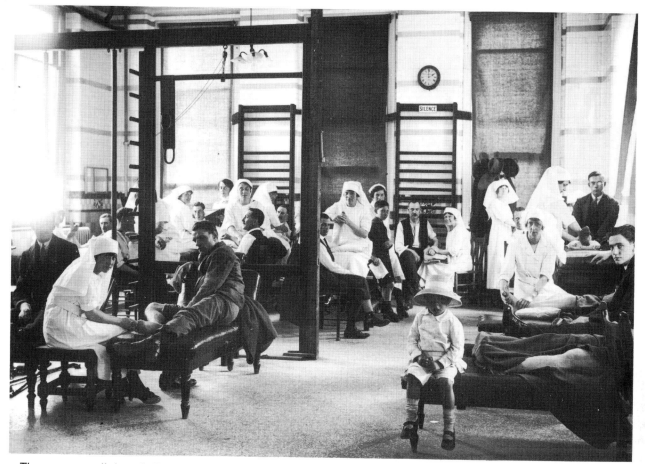

The massage clinic at St Bartholomew's Hospital, London, one of Britain's oldest hospitals. Hospitals like this had always admitted patients free of charge, but after the war, they began to have difficulty in finding the money they needed. Why would there have been a particular demand for massage clinics after the war? Note the electric light fixture.

## THE WEEKLY BILL OF FARE AT AN INTERMEDIATE SCHOOL IN SOUTH WALES

| | |
|---|---|
| Monday | Hot pot; roly-poly pudding. |
| Tuesday | Joint, vegetables and potatoes; prunes and rice. |
| Wednesday | Liver and bacon; suet pudding and syrup. |
| Thursday | Joint, vegetables and potatoes; tinned apricots and custard. |
| Friday | Hot pot; pineapple and custard. |

From the *Report of the Board of Education, 1926)*

How does this menu compare with your school meals service?

## WORK WITH MOTHERS AND BABIES

The Ministry of Health also encouraged local councils to set up mother and baby clinics. This notice appeared in the *Old Oak Tenants' Association Newsletter* in February 1929.

There must be many mothers new to the district who do not know that twice a week ... the Old Oak branch of the Hammersmith Welfare Centre meets at St Catherine's Hall, ready to help mothers and babies with advice and sympathy. A warm welcome is given to all mothers who will come to see the work that is being done for mothers and babies in this district.

# Food Changes

During the Twenties the food that people ate and their way of buying it began to change. Although food rations were ended in 1920, progress was fairly slow, and it was not until the Thirties that Cornflakes and other breakfast foods, and tinned products such as fish and vegetables, became common articles of diet. There were no frozen foods in the Twenties, but more varieties of jellies, biscuits and sweets were coming into the shops. As we saw on page 26, one million packets of Smith's potato crisps were sold in 1928.

## THE CORNER SHOP

Before the coming of buses and cars and the opening of new "chain" shops in the towns, most people bought things at the shop on the corner of their street, like this one in St Helen's, described by one of the shopkeeper's daughters,

> We lived at Robins Lane and had a grocery shop. We had an outdoor licence and sold beer at fourpence a quart. Children used to come for a gill [half a pint] on Sundays and we used to give them sweets. Inside we sold nearly everything . . . on Tuesdays, Wednesdays and Thursdays we sold fish. We sold cigarettes at twopence halfpenny a packet and tobacco at threepence an ounce. We sold writing paper at a halfpenny a sheet, penny bottles of turpentine, headache powders, pills and settlers powders at twopence halfpenny. When the Co-op opened it took our trade away . . .

(Quoted in C.F. Forman, ed., *Industrial Town: Self Portrait of St Helens in the 1920s*, 1979)

What age do you have to be before you can buy beer in a shop nowadays? What sort of things does a grocer sell today? List the advantages and disadvantages of a corner shop as compared with a supermarket.

## MILK

At this time a new method of delivering milk to customers in the town came into use. Instead of buying milk in a jug, ladled out of a large churn from

*A Sainsbury's branch shop opened at Croydon in 1930. Branches opened in the Twenties had similar tiles on the walls and floor. Notice the packets of tea and the tins of salmon on the shelves. Butter was still cut off a large slab by the pound or half pound.*

Many of the old-fashioned butchers shops still remained, like this one in Banbury Road, Oxford. ◇◇◇ Notice the joints of meat hanging up outside the shop. Now we do not approve of this. Why not? Notice Mr Howard's delivery van.

the back of a cart, it could now be delivered to your doorstep, sealed up in a bottle, as this account from a magazine shows.

> The London Co-op Dairy at Oakthorpe Park is now sending out over 100,000 bottles of sanitised milk every week. New plant has been installed bringing the capacity up to 400 gallons per hour. Over twenty vans are delivering in north London and lorry-loads are being sent into the west. The total sales of the London Co-op are upwards of 50,000 gallons a week. We believe this to be a record. (*The London Citizen*, June 1922)

Why should this way of delivering milk be an improvement? Do you still have milk delivered to your door at home?

## CAREFUL HOUSEKEEPING

Although there was real hunger amongst striking miners and their families and the unemployed, a family on low wages could manage if the mother was a careful housekeeper. Albert Twigg, who grew up in a poor family in Middlesex, described how his family were fed in an interview with Wembley Historical Society in 1982.

> On Saturday night we went to the butchers and bought an aitch bone [rump] of beef at cut price. There was no refrigeration [in shops] then and

## IMPROVED PHYSIQUE

The effect of better food on the health of young people is shown in this report from the Ministry of Health in 1927.

> Comment had been made by several of the . . . surgeons on the improved health of young people presenting themselves for examination. Dr Trimble of Bamber Bridge adds, the physique of girls far exceeds that of boys. . . . He comments on the prevalence of smoking amongst boys. (*Ministry of Health Report*, 1927)

Smoking seems to have been on the increase amongst young working-class men, perhaps because of increased wages during the war. What do we know these days about the health risks of smoking?

> butchers always sold off their meat cheaply on Saturday night. We always had beef roasted on Sunday, served cold on Monday, rissoles on Tuesday, cottage pie on Wednesday, pasties etc. on Thursdays. Anyhow, it lasted all the week . . . and the procedure was the same every week.
>
> We also had large amounts of bread and dripping, and bread and treacle. Beef dripping and treacle were considered good for us and I can remember eating four or five slices of bread and this stuff at a sitting. My mother also made suet pudding to fill us up. For tea (on Sunday), there was always plenty of bread and butter, a bowl of tinned fruit and evaporated milk.

Would we consider this an adequate diet today?

# At School

By the end of the war many children, unless their parents could afford fees for their private education, left school at 14 or even earlier. It was generally felt that all children should stay at school until 15 and be given the same chance of learning as fee-paying children, but in the troubled times of the Twenties not enough money could be found for such a scheme. Nevertheless, some progress was made towards better education for everyone. Some county councils provided secondary schools for their pupils who passed a scholarship examination, and some bright children were able to take up a free place at their local grammar school.

## AT THE GRAMMAR SCHOOL

Gerry Carthew, who was born in Canada and came to live in Hastings between the wars, describes his education at the local grammar school.

> I went to the grammar school when we came to Hastings, as a fee-payer. I think it cost about a tenner a term . . . . Scholarships were restricted to boys who had been to elementary schools in the town. I think, by and large, scholarship boys were brighter than the fee-payers. You could tell who were the scholarship boys because, in those days, fee-payers started off in form 1, and scholarship boys went into 2a. I started in form 1 . . . but after a term I was pushed up to form 2a with the scholarship boys. I was the only fee-payer in the class. There was no discrimination either for or against scholarship boys . . . . The only difference I noticed personally was that when I went there I had covered a lot more subjects. I had done a little bit of Greek, I'd done Latin and algebra, which weren't touched at all until the third form of the grammar school. I had done these subjects at a fee-paying school in Eastbourne before I came to Hastings. (Quoted in *Hastings Voices*, 1982)

Find out if there were scholarship places at your school. If there were, when did the system change? Does anyone in your school study Greek or Latin.?

## A CENTRAL SCHOOL FOR GIRLS

In the past, education for girls had been rather neglected. It was not considered necessary to give them as much education as their brothers. In the central and high schools built in the Twenties, although boys and girls still went to separate schools, attempts were made to give girls a wider and more varied programme, as this report, made on 15 April 1927 by a member of the Local Education Committee in South London shows:

> With my daughter I devoted this afternoon to visiting the Girls' Central School. I was most impressed by the keenness of both staff and pupils . . . . Handwriting was quite up to the mark . . . . In one classroom, where girls were studying English, we were treated to a recital of Shelley's "Ode to the West Wind", given with taste and expression . . . . Practical science was being taught in another room. The girls learn domestic science in their first three years at the Central School and this together with sewing lessons should fit them to be good economic housewives.

What do you think the visitor thought was the most important things the girls were learning? Do you agree with that?

The importance of introducing children to a healthy diet was being recognized in the Twenties. Here the boys and girls of St Ignatius' Catholic school are being given a "good fairy" lecture as part of the National Milk Publicity Campaign of 1925. What sort of food is the good fairy approving? Boys and girls were split into separate classes for lessons.

The netball team at Chislehurst Road school in Kent. Do you think you would have been comfortable playing netball in such clothes? Notice the wide bands they are wearing.

## THE HUMAN FACE OF ARITHMETIC

Teaching methods in the Twenties were often very formal and rather dull compared with today, though some attempts were made to make things more interesting. Edward Blishen, who left his Barley Lane school in 1929, recalls his arithmetic lessons:

> I think now what a solemn school it was compared with any primary school today . . . . In arithmetic we did so much division of unlikely numbers and quantities; though there was I see, looking through an old exercise book, some attempt to give arithmetic a human face. The sum, 350 x 6, would have the heading "bricks"; not plain numbers but bricks, pigs or cakes. Someone had 5735 cakes to be divided into four heaps. An imaginary farmer had a quarter of a pig left over on his farm in my exercise book on March 18th 1928. (Edward Blishen, *Sorry Dad. Good Times at Home*, 1978)

Do you think that Edward Blishen had got his sum wrong to have a quarter of a pig left over?

# Sports and Entertainment

Many of the games and entertainments which became popular in the Twenties had been played for a long time before the war; but the coming of the motor car, more leisure time and a higher standard of living made it possible for more people to take part, or at least to watch other people perform.

## THE CINEMA

After the war the cinema provided a popular form of entertainment. Going to the pictures became a regular habit for thousands of people who for as little as sixpence (less than 3p), could follow the adventures of their favourite film stars in the comfort of the rather grand cinema halls which were springing up everywhere. Some towns would have as many as four or five picture palaces, as they were called; and most of them would be full, especially on Saturday nights. Mrs Florence Smith, who lived in a small Wiltshire village, remembers her Saturday visit to the cinema.

We had no radio; the only entertainment we had was the cinema in a town about three miles away where we went on Saturdays to sit and gaze in rapture at the wonderful film star of the day, Rudolph Valentino. We girls fell desperately in love with him. I don't know what it was about him; he couldn't even talk to us in those far-off silent days, but oh, how we did love him. . . . I remember him as an Arab in a tent, kissing a girl he had carried off . . . the film of "The Sheik" to me, as a film fan, was just IT.

The outing to the Picture Palace was an adventure, not only for the films we saw . . . we went into town in a wagonette drawn by two trotting horses; it was great fun. (Quoted in Lesley Bailey and C.H. Brewer, eds., *BBC Scrapbook for 1922*, 1937)

There are three things in that passage that tell you it was *early* in the Twenties. Can you spot them?

*Charlie Chaplin was one of the most famous comedians of the Twenties. Thousands of people flocked to see his films like* The Gold Rush *and* The Kid, *which he made with a child star, Jackie Coogan.*

## GOLF

Before the war, golf had been the sport of kings and the aristocracy, but in the Twenties many middle-class people – such as doctors, lawyers and businessmen – took up the game. By 1929 at least 25 new courses had opened within 50 miles of London alone. Often country houses which were for sale were used as clubhouses for the golfers. This article from the introduction to a golfers' handbook explains the reason for the increased number of golfers.

> **Golf and motoring are clearly allied. The golfer is nearly always a motorist and has come to regard the possession of a car as nearly indispensable to the pursuit of his hobby. A golf course distant five, ten or fifteen miles is nowadays, in this motor-minded age, as good as on your door-step. Twenty five miles is a pleasant run, and fifty should see even the world's worst early riser on the first teeing green by 11 a.m.**
> (Quoted in English Golf Union, *Fifty Miles of Golf Around London*, 1937)

Although this book was published in 1937, already in the Twenties the number of golfers and courses for them to use was growing fast. Is there a golf course near you? Find out when it was built.

◁ *Football increased in popularity in the Twenties. When the first cup final was played at the Wembley stadium in 1923 so many people flocked on to the pitch that the game was held up for over half an hour. In the match Bolton Wanderers beat West Ham.*

## THE MIGHTY ONE

A young man who could not afford a car could sometimes afford a second-hand motor bike, as Albert Edward Trigg recalled in a recorded interview in 1979:

> **By 1927 I was able to buy myself a second-hand motor bike and I went a good few miles on that . . . . In 1929 I bought a Rudge Ulster, which was the latest machine at the time. It had four valves and four speeds. I called it the MIGHTY ONE.**
>
> **I used to go to Bournemouth on this machine on Sundays in the summer. First I went with my friend Jack . . . who was very keen on dirt-track racing; he had a girl friend and when I met Rima in 1929 the four of us used to go out together with the two girls on the pillion . . . . We often had a terrible job to get home, there was so much traffic on the road. We used to weave in and out; how we weren't killed I don't know.**

Racing on motor bikes was a very popular sport with young men at the time. What safety items do motorcyclists wear today?

# Holidays and Outings

## A CARAVAN HOLIDAY

Caravans, which first came on the market in about 1922, could provide for those who wanted to spend a little more time on the road. The first trailer caravans were rather heavy and clumsy, being modelled on the old horse-drawn vehicles. Leslie Bailey took one on his honeymoon.

> With what affection do I remember the Eccles caravan with its lantern roof, the lower edges of which seemed to collide with my head every day during the honeymoon trip we took from Yorkshire to Cornwall and back in 1928. Caravans were rare, we saw only three during our three week holiday of over 1500 miles. Our caravan was drawn by a Morris Cowley open two seater. There were no caravan parks. Farmers everywhere gave us permission to park in their fields overnight. Most of them refused payment. (Quoted in Leslie Bailey and C.H. Brewer, eds., *BBC Scrapbook*, 1937)

For many middle-class families a fortnight in a boarding house at the seaside was the usual way to spend the summer holiday, but more and more people were able to take a few extra days off work. Motor picnics were a popular day's outing for those with private transport, while for those who could afford a cheap ticket on a train, rambling, or hiking, was a pleasant way of exploring the countryside.

## RESTFUL AND HAPPY EXPERIENCES

There were no cheap package tours abroad in the Twenties, but for those who could afford it, travelling abroad could be both comfortable and amusing, as C.V. Buckley records in *Good Times at Home and Abroad*, published in 1979:

> In 1921 I went to China . . . on a slow boat; a small P.&O. liner, the SS Dongola. As far as I can remember it took about six weeks with stops at ports along the way . . . . These ports of call were long enough to allow passengers to go ashore and see the sights.

Picnics in the countryside were popular with city-dwellers. These two couples seem to be very well-organized! Notice the caravan in the background.

Hop-pickers at work on a farm near Tonbridge in Kent. In the background you can see the chimneys of the oast houses in which the hops were dried.

Every evening we changed into evening clothes for dinner; we played a lot of deck games and had ship's concerts . . .

Now it is possible to fly to China. Can you find out how long it takes by air?

## A WORKING HOLIDAY IN KENT

In September every year thousands of working-class families from London made their way into the Kentish countryside for a hop-picking holiday. In an interview given specially for this book Wilfred Ralph, who grew up in a small village near Maidstone, remembers the arrival of the "East-Enders", as they were called, at the hop farms in the neighbourhood.

They came every year in September, often to the same farm, bringing with them cooking stoves, kitchen utensils, everything the family would need for a month. They stayed until the harvest ended in October. The huts provided for them would be called primitive by today's standards. They had to bring their own bedding, and if it was cold at night, as it could be in September, the whole family would huddle together on one mattress for warmth and comfort. There was no hot water at most camps. All water supplies had to be taken from a stand-pipe and boiled on a stove.

The whole family came; it was usually the only holiday they had. The money they earned was to buy extras for the children – boots and warm winter coats. All the family, even quite small children, would help with the picking. It wasn't difficult but the hops were very light and a lot were needed to fill the baskets, or bins, as they were called . . . .

The Londoners were welcome for the money they brought to the pubs and the village shop. There would be an occasional fight, but not much violence. We children rather enjoyed the excitement, but I think that some of the older people in the village were shocked by their rowdiness and bad language. We also had gypsies, in their painted caravans, but these had to be kept separate. They worked in a different hop field.

What would the hops have been used for? Are hops still picked by hand? What kinds of working holidays are popular today?

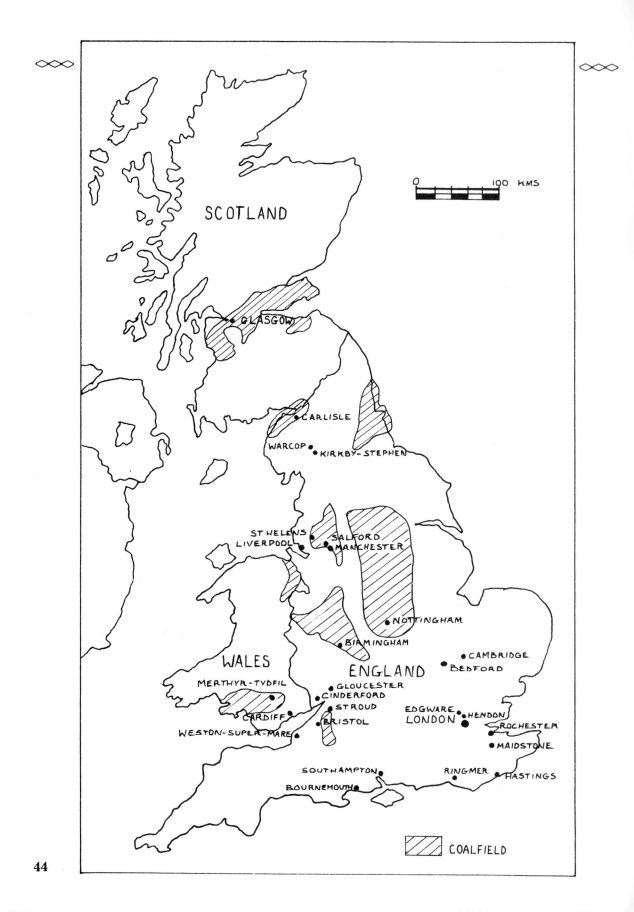

SCOTLAND

GLASGOW

100 KMS

CARLISLE

WARCOP
KIRKBY-STEPHEN

ST HELENS
LIVERPOOL
SALFORD
MANCHESTER

NOTTINGHAM

BIRMINGHAM

WALES
CAMBRIDGE
BEDFORD

MERTHYR-TYDFIL
ENGLAND

GLOUCESTER
CINDERFORD
STROUD
CARDIFF
BRISTOL
EDGWARE
LONDON
HENDON
ROCHESTER

WESTON-SUPER-MARE
MAIDSTONE

SOUTHAMPTON
RINGMER
HASTINGS

BOURNEMOUTH

COALFIELD

# Difficult Words

| | |
|---|---|
| angler | a fisherman who uses a rod and line. |
| armistice | a temporary lull in the fighting; a truce. |
| avant-garde | ahead of the times; a leader of fashion. |
| bankrupt | to be unable to pay debts; a business failure. |
| Charleston | a fast dance with kicks out to the side. Named after Charleston in the United States. |
| dole | common name for money paid to the unemployed. |
| eucalyptus oil | oil from the leaves of an Australian tree; used for medical purposes. |
| flapper | a young woman in the Twenties who wore unusual clothes and cut her hair short; one of the Bright Young Things. |
| genial | a pleasant, friendly person. |
| gill | a liquid measure, equalling 5fl.oz, or one-quarter of a pint. In Northern dialect it is half a pint and is used especially of beer. |
| jaunty | carefree. |
| jiggered | here it means tired out. |
| Monsoon | an Asian wind which brings the rainy season. |
| Oxford Bags | trousers with very wide legs, fashionable in the Twenties. |
| piecework | work paid by the number of articles produced. |
| pike | large freshwater fish. |
| pillion | pad or cushion for a passenger on the back of a motor bike. |
| plus-fours | knickerbockers bagging below the knee. Worn by men when playing golf. |
| quart | liquid measure equal to two pints. |
| Savile Row | Street in London's Mayfair where fashionable young men had their clothes made by a tailor. |
| Season, London | The period from May to July when the fashionable world was in residence and when young women (débutantes) were introduced at Court and launched into Society. |
| standpipe | vertical pipe with a tap to provide water when there was no mains supply. |
| surplice | loose white robe worn by clergy of the Church of England. |
| tarpaulin | waterproof canvas used to protect goods against damp. |
| tuberculosis | an infectious disease common in the nineteenth century caused by bad living conditions. |
| unchaperoned | without the usual relative or friend who accompanied young unmarried girls to parties, etc. |
| wagonette | a horse-drawn passenger vehicle with seats for about ten people facing each other. |

**Money**
Always look at what money and wages could buy rather than at what seem low prices to us. It is no use butter being 4p a pound if we only earn 50p a week. Remember that there were 12 old pence (d.) in a shilling (s.) and 20 shillings to the pound. 6d. was the equivalent of 2½p, a shilling (1/-) 5p.

# Date List

| | |
|---|---|
| **1920** | War-time food rationing ends. |
| *16 June* | First wireless concert broadcast; Melba sings. |
| *31 August* | War officially ends. |
| *11 November* | King George V unveils Cenotaph, memorial to war dead. |
| | |
| **1921** | Miners go on strike. |
| | National Insurance Act gives 15s. (75p) per week to unemployed. |
| | First all-electric house on exhibition in London. |
| | Austin 7, the first mass-produced car on sale. |
| *7 August* | Zeppelin R38 crashes over the Humber. |
| | |
| **1922** | British Broadcasting Company set up. |
| | Slump in economy; unemployment grows. |
| *November* | Conservatives win General Election. |
| | |
| **1923** | |
| *January* | Unemployed demonstration in London. |
| *23 April* | Princess Mary marries Earl of Harewood. |
| *May* | Stanley Baldwin becomes Prime Minister. |
| *October* | 160,000 people see first football cup tie at Wembley. |
| *December* | Labour wins General Election; Ramsey Macdonald Prime Minister. |
| | |
| **1924** | |
| *January* | Strike on railways. |
| *23 April* | Great Empire Exhibition opened at Wembley; King's voice recorded for first time. |
| *October* | Conservatives win General Election; Stanley Baldwin Prime Minister. |
| | |
| **1925** | First traffic lights installed in London. |
| *April* | Empire Exhibition opened for second year. |
| | Greyhound racing at Wembley. |
| | |
| **1926** | |
| *4-12 May* | General Strike. |
| | Alan Cobham's flight to Australia ends at Westminster. |
| | First houses built on Watling Estate by LCC. |
| | Central Electricity Board set up. |
| | Imperial Chemical Industries founded. |
| | |
| **1927** | First automatic telephone exchange. |
| | First television demonstration. |
| | Croydon Airport opened. |
| | |
| **1928** | Women to vote at 21. |
| | "Talkies" in cinema. |
| | |
| **1929** | |
| *May* | Macdonald heads second Labour government after General Election. |
| | R101 launched. |
| | Amy Johnson qualifies as air pilot. |
| | Collapse of American Banks leads to Great Depression. |

# Biographical Notes

ASTOR Lady Nancy (born Nancy Langhorne, 19 May 1879, Virginia, USA). Came to England in 1904. Married Waldorf Astor, an English Member of Parliament. After the Great War, when her husband became a peer, Lady Astor succeeded him as M.P. for Plymouth. She was the first woman to take her seat in the House of Commons. She held Plymouth for the Conservatives until the Second World War, when she retired from politics. Lady Astor was a supporter of the temperance movement, which preached abstinence from alcohol, and a supporter of women's rights. She died on 2 May 1964, aged 84.

BALDWIN Stanley (born 1867). The son of a Worcestershire iron-master, Stanley Baldwin was educated at Harrow and Cambridge. He became Member of Parliament for Bewdley in 1908, Financial Secretary to the Treasury in 1917, President of the Board of Trade from 1921 to 1922, Chancellor of the Exchequer from 1922 to 1923, and Prime Minister in 1923, 1924-9 and 1935-7. He was responsible for handling the General Strike and the Abdication Crisis. He retired from politics in 1937 and was created Lord Bewdley. He died in 1947.

MACDONALD James Ramsay (born 1866 at Lossiemouth, Scotland). The son of a poor family, he came to London at the age of 19. He joined the Labour Party, and became leader in 1911. He was a pacifist during the Great War years. He was Prime Minister of the first Labour Government in 1924, and again in 1929. He was leader of a National Government between 1931 and 1935 with the Conservatives. He died in 1937 while cruising for the sake of his health.

LEE Laurie (born 1915 in Gloucestershire). He has published several books of poetry and prose, including an account of Spain during the Civil War. *Cider with Rosie*, an account of his childhood in a small village, won him a literary award. He now lives in London and enjoys travelling and music.

RIDER-HAGGARD Sir Henry (born 1856, in Norfolk). Educated privately and at Cambridge, he served with the British administration in South Africa. He studied Law on his return to England and travelled in many parts of the world. He wrote a number of novels. The best remembered – *King Solomon's Mines, Alan Quartermaine* and *She* – are all set in Africa. Sir Henry was knighted in 1912. He died in 1924.

SHORT Edward Watson (born 1912, in Cuberian Village of Warcop). Educated locally and at Durham University and London, Edward Short served in the army during the war. After a teaching career and serving as leader of the Labour Group on Newcastle City Council, he became M.P. for Newcastle on Tyne. He served as Secretary of State for Education and Science in 1968 and as Leader of the House of Commons in 1974. In 1977 he was made a Baron and became Lord Glenamara. He now lives at Corbridge, Northumberland. His hobby is painting.

People who gave an interview for this book:

GULLIVER Dorothy. Dorothy was born in North London and began her education at Noel Park Mixed Infants school where the Empire Day ceremonies took place. She went on to a local grammar school and then to the University of London. After qualifying as a teacher Dorothy held a number of posts in different schools before becoming a lecturer in English at a College of Education. Dorothy is retired now, and lives with her husband at Battle in Sussex.

RALPH Wilfred. Wilfred was born in Frittenden, a Kent village near Maidstone. Educated at Cranbrook School, then training as a teacher, Wilfred served in the RAF during the war, before starting his teaching career. After teaching at Hastings Grammar School for 25 years, he went on to become Deputy Head of a comprehensive school. He taught sports and English. Wilfred and his family live at Hastings, Sussex.

# Book List

Michael Anglo, *Spotlight on the Twenties* (Jupiter Books, 1976)

Lesley Bailey and C.H. Brewer (eds.) *B.B.C. Scrapbook*, Vol. 2 (Hutchinson, 1937; Allen and Unwin, 1969).

Richard Bennet, *A Picture of the Twenties* (Vesta Books, 1961)

S.E. Ellacott, *A History of Everyday Things in England*, Vol. V 1914-1968 (Batsford, 1968)

Winifred Foley, *A Child in the Forest* (Futura, 1974)

Rose Gamble, *Chelsea Child* (Ariel Books, BBC, 1979)

M.V. Hughes, *A London Family Between the Wars,* (Oxford University Press, 1979)

Laurie Lee, *Cider with Rosie* (Penguin, 1959)

Jean Metcalfe, *Sunnylea, A 1920's Childhood Remembered* (Michael Joseph, 1980)

Graham Mitchell, *Living Through History: The Roaring Twenties* (Batsford, 1986)

J. Montgomery, *The Twenties* (Allen and Unwin, 1970)

L.C.B. Seaman, *Life in Britain between the Wars* (Batsford, 1970)

R.J. Unstead, *The Twenties: 1919-1929* (Macdonald Educational, 1973)

Frances Wilkins, *Growing up Between the Wars* (Batsford, 1979)

# Index